D1462976

# THE GREAT
# INFIDELS

# THE GREAT
# INFIDELS

# ROBERT INGERSOLL

American Atheist Press, P.O. Box 5733, Parsippany, NJ 07054-6733

© 1982, 1990 by American Atheist Press. All rights reserved.
Published 1982. Revised Edition 1990. Reprinted March 2000.
Printed in the United States of America.

**Library of Congress Cataloging-in-Publication Data**

Ingersoll, Robert Green, 1833 -1899.
The great infidels / by Robert Ingersoll ; with a foreword by Jon G.
Murray. — 2nd ed.
   p.   cm.
Rev. ed. of: What great infidels have done to advance civilization.
c1982.
Includes bibliographical references.
ISBN 0-910309-08-6 (paperback)
   1. Free thought—History. 2. Civilization, Occidental.
I. Ingersoll, Robert Green, 1833-1899. What great infidels have
done to advance civilization. II. Title.
BL2725.W35 1990                             90.40641
   211'.7'09—dc20                                  CIP

# Contents

# Foreword

Perhaps the single question which Atheists are asked more often than any other is: "What would the world be like without religion?" This is coupled with the obvious follow-up: "Whence would we derive our morals?" Inherent in both questions is the acceptance of the false premise that all morality is based on religion, or – alternatively – that humankind's present condition comes from its roots in religion.

Of course, the Atheist would agree that all which is bad in our culture does come from religion. The theist, in posing his question, posits that all that is good in our culture comes from religion.

The art of "the big lie" is demonstrated in this dilemma, for the religious community has convinced all of humankind of an asset which it purports to have but which, indeed, never accrued to religion, except for the claiming of it.

Robert G. Ingersoll, "the Great Agnostic," saw this clearly and set about to show that the ingrained idea of the superiority of religion as a basis for ethics or morality was, simply, false. Taking as basis for his remarks the life and the achievements of just a few great men – Julian, Bruno, Voltaire, Diderot, Hume, and Spinoza from European countries, and Paine, Franklin, and Jefferson from our own – he elaborates on the thesis of theism versus non-theism. His dramatic language and breadth of thought sweep one into the excitement of the ideas he embraces and proposes. Truth, after all, is a sharp cutting knife, and the exhilaration which comes from it an aid to mental stimulation. The excitement is on every page one reads.

But Ingersoll also faces the giant arguments which have impeded the progress of humankind: the revered dead with, necessarily, the intact ideas of those dead; the display of martyrs who, having died for their ideas, should make those ideas sacrosanct, willy-nilly, whether good or bad.

Ingersoll would have nothing of sham, nothing of hypocrisy, nothing of deceit. He is, today, as much of an inspiration to all mankind as he tried to be in his life. Once introduced to Ingersoll, one cannot forget him, or cast him aside. His arguments are too compelling; his language is too beautifully precise; his logic is too impeccable.

As you come to the reading of this small booklet, find yourself a comfortable chair, relax – you are about to have the time of your intellectual life. When you get up, you will be a wiser human.

Jon G. Murray

# The Great Infidels

*This lecture is printed from notes found among Robert G. Ingersoll's papers, but not revised by him for publication.*

I have sometimes thought that it will not make great and splendid character to rock children in the cradle of hypocrisy. I do not believe that the tendency is to make men and women brave and glorious when you tell them that there are certain ideas upon certain subjects that they must never express; that they must go through life with a pretense as a shield; that their neighbors will think much more of them if they will only keep still; and that above all is a God who despises one who honestly expresses what he believes. For my part, I believe men will be nearer honest in business, in politics, grander in art – in everything that is good and grand and beautiful, if they are taught from the cradle to the coffin to tell their honest opinion.

Neither do I believe thought to be dangerous. It is incredible that only idiots are absolutely sure of salvation. It is incredible that the more brain you have the less your chance is. There can be no danger in honest thought, and if the world ever advances beyond what it is today, it must be led by men who express their real opinions.

We have passed midnight in the great struggle between Fact and Faith, between Science and Superstition. The brand of intellectual inferiority is now upon the orthodox brain. There is nothing grander than to rescue from the leprosy of slander the reputation of a good and generous man. Nothing can be nearer just than to benefit our benefactors.

The Infidels of one age have been the aureoled saints of the next. The destroyers of the old are the creators of the new. The old passes away, and the new becomes old. There is in the intellectual world, as in the material, decay and growth, and ever by the grave of buried age stand youth and joy.

The history of intellectual progress is written in the lives of Infidels. Political rights have been preserved by traitors – the liberty of the mind by heretics. To attack the king was treason – to dispute the priest was blasphemy. The sword and cross were allies. They defended each other. The throne and altar were twins – vultures from the same egg.

It was James I who said: "No bishop, no king." He might have said: "No cross, no crown."

The king owned the bodies, and the priest the souls, of men. One lived on taxes, the other on alms. One was a robber, the other a beggar, and each was both.

These robbers and beggars controlled two worlds. The king made laws, the priest made creeds. With bowed backs the people received the burdens of the one, and with wonder's open mouth the dogmas of the other. If any aspired to be free they were crushed by the king, and every priest was a Herod who slaughtered the children of the brain. The king ruled by force, the priest by fear, and both by both.

The king said to the people: "God made you peasants, and he made me king. He made rags and hovels for you, robes and palaces for me. Such is the justice of God." And the priest said: "God made you ignorant and vile. He made me holy and wise. If you do not obey me, God will punish you here and torment you hereafter. Such is the mercy of God."

Infidels are intellectual discoverers. They sail the unknown seas and find new isles and continents in the infinite realms of thought.

An Infidel is one who has found a new fact, who has an idea of his own, and who in the mental sky has seen another star.

He is an intellectual capitalist, and for that reason excites the envy and hatred of the theological pauper.

2

# The Origin of God and Heaven, of the Devil and Hell

In the estimation of good orthodox Christians I am a criminal, because I am trying to take from loving mothers, fathers, brothers, sisters, husbands, wives, and lovers the consolations naturally arising from a belief in an eternity of grief and pain. I want to tear, break, and scatter to the winds the God that priests erected in the fields of innocent pleasure – a God made of sticks called creeds, and of old clothes called myths. I shall endeavor to take from the coffin its horror, from the cradle its curse, and put out the fires of revenge kindled by an infinite fiend.

Is it necessary that heaven should borrow its light from the glare of hell?

Infinite punishment is infinite cruelty, endless injustice, immortal meanness. To worship an eternal gaoler hardens, debases, and pollutes even the vilest soul. While there is one sad and breaking heart in the universe, no good being can be perfectly happy.

Against the heartlessness of the Christian religion every grand and tender soul should enter solemn protest. The God of hell should be held in loathing, contempt, and scorn. A God who threatens eternal pain should be hated, not loved – cursed, not worshiped. A heaven presided over by such a God must be below the lowest hell. I want no part in any heaven in which the saved, the ransomed, and redeemed will drown with shouts of joy the cries and sobs of hell – in which happiness will forget misery, where the tears of the lost only increase laughter and double bliss.

The idea of hell was born of ignorance, brutality, fear, cowardice, and revenge. This idea testifies that our remote ancestors were the lowest beasts. Only from dens, lairs, and caves, only from mouths filled with cruel fangs, only from hearts of fear and hatred, only from the conscience of hunger and lust, only from the lowest and most debased could come this most cruel, heartless, and bestial of all dogmas.

Our barbarian ancestors knew but little of nature. They were too astonished to investigate. They could not divest themselves of the idea that everything happened with reference to them; that they caused storms and earthquakes; that they brought the tempest and the whirlwind; that on account of something they had done, or omitted to do, the lightning of vengeance leaped from the darkened sky. They made up their minds that at least two vast and powerful beings presided over this world; that one was good and the other bad; that both of these beings wished to get control of the souls of men; that they were relentless enemies, eternal foes; that both welcomed recruits and hated deserters; that both demanded praise and worship; that one offered rewards in this world, and the other in the next. The Devil has paid cash – God buys on credit.

Man saw cruelty and mercy in nature, because he imagined that phenomena were produced to punish or to reward him. When his poor hut was torn and broken by the wind, he thought it a punishment. When some town or city was swept away by flood or sea, he imagined that the crimes of the inhabitants had been avenged. When the land was filled with plenty, when the seasons were kind, he thought that he had pleased the tyrant of the skies.

It must be remembered that both gods and devils were supposed to be presided over by the greatest God and the greatest Devil. The God could give infinite rewards and could inflict infinite torments. The Devil could assist man here; could give him wealth and place in this world, in consideration of owning his soul hereafter. Each human soul was a prize contended for by these deities. Of course this God and this Devil

4

had innumerable spirits at their command, to execute their decrees. The God lived in heaven and the Devil in hell. Both were monarchs and were infinitely jealous of each other. The priests pretended to be the agents and recruiting sergeants of this God, and they were duly authorized to promise and threaten in his name; they had power to forgive and curse. These priests sought to govern the world by force and fear. Believing that men could be frightened into obedience, they magnified the tortures and terrors of perdition. Believing also that man could in part be influenced by the hope of reward, they magnified the joys of heaven. In other words, they promised eternal joy and threatened everlasting pain. Most of these priests, born of the ignorance of the time, believed what they taught. They proved that God was good, by sunlight and harvest, by health and happiness; that he was angry, by disease and death. Man, according to this doctrine, was led astray by the Devil, who delighted only in evil. It was supposed that God demanded worship; that he loved to be flattered; that he delighted in sacrifice; that nothing made him happier than to see ignorant faith upon its knees; that above all things he hated and despised doubters and heretics, and that he regarded all investigation as rebellion.

Now and then believers in these ideas, those who had gained great reputation for learning and sanctity, or had enjoyed great power, wrote books, and these books after a time were considered sacred. Most of them were written to frighten mankind, and were filled with threatenings and curses for unbelievers and promises for the faithful. The more frightful the curses, the more extravagant the promises, the more sacred the books were considered. All of the gods were cruel and vindictive, unforgiving and relentless, and the devils were substantially the same.

It was also believed that certain things must be accepted as true, no matter whether they were reasonable or not; that it was pleasing to God to believe a certain creed, especially if it happened to be the creed of the majority. Each community felt it a duty to see that the enemies of God were converted or killed. To allow a heretic to live in peace was to invite the wrath of God. Every public evil – every misfortune – was accounted for by something the community had permitted or done. When epidemics appeared, brought by ignorance and welcomed by filth, the heretic was brought out and sacrificed to appease the vengeance of God. From the knowledge they had – from their premises – they reasoned well. They said, If God will inflict such frightful torments upon us here, simply for allowing a few heretics to live, what will he do with the heretics? Of course the heretics would be punished forever. They knew how cruel was the barbarian king when he had the traitor in his power. They had seen every horror that man could inflict on man. Of course a God could do more than a king. He could punish forever. The fires he would kindle never could be quenched. The torments he would inflict would be eternal. They thought the amount of punishment would be measured only by the power of God.

These ideas were not only prevalent in what are called barbarous times, but they are received by the religious world of today.

No death could be conceived more horrible than that produced by flames. To these flames they added eternity, and hell was produced. They exhausted the idea of personal torture.

By putting intention behind what man called good, God was produced. By putting intention behind what man called bad, the Devil was created. Leave this "intention" out, and gods and devils fade away.

If not a human being existed the sun would continue to shine, and tempests now and then would devastate the world; the rain would fall in pleasant showers, and the bow of promise would adorn the cloud; violets would spread their velvet bosoms to the sun, and the earthquake would devour; birds would sing, and daisies bloom, and roses blush, and the volcanoes would fill the heavens with their lurid glare; the procession of the seasons would not be broken, and the stars would shine just as serenely as though the world was filled with loving hearts and happy homes. But in the olden time man thought otherwise. He imagined that he was of great importance. Barbarians are always egotistic. They think that the stars are watching them; that the sun shines on their account; that the rain falls for them, and that gods and devils are really troubling themselves about their poor and ignorant souls.

In those days men fought for their God as they did for their king. They killed the enemies of both. For this their king would reward them here, and their God hereafter. With them it was loyalty to destroy the disloyal. They did not regard God as a vague "spirit," nor as an "essence" without body or parts, but as a being, a person, an infinite man, a king, the monarch of the universe, who had garments of glory for believers and robes of flame for the heretic and Infidel.

Do not imagine that this doctrine of hell belongs to Christianity alone. Nearly all religions have had this dogma for a cornerstone. Upon this burning foundation nearly all have built. Over the abyss of pain rose the glittering dome of pleasure. This world was regarded as one of trial. Here a God of infinite wisdom experimented with man. Between the outstretched paws of the Infinite the mouse, man, was allowed to play. Here man had the opportunity of hearing priests and kneeling in temples. Here he could read and hear read the sacred books. Here he could have the example of the pious and the counsels of the holy. Here he could build churches and cathedrals. Here he could burn incense, fast, wear haircloth, deny himself all the pleasures of life, confess to priests, count beads, be miserable one day in seven, make creeds, construct instruments of torture, bow before pictures and images, eat little square pieces of bread, sprinkle water on the heads of babes, shut his eyes and say words to the clouds, and slander and defame all who have the courage to despise superstition, and the goodness to tell their honest thoughts. After death, nothing could be done to make him better. When he should come into the presence of God, nothing was left except to damn him. Priests might convert him here, but God could do nothing there – all of which shows how much more a priest can do for a soul than its creator; how much more potent is the example of your average Christian than that of all the angels, and how much superior earth is to heaven for the moral development of the soul. In heaven the Devil is not allowed to enter. There all are pure and perfect, yet they cannot influence a soul for good.

Only here, on the earth, where the Devil is constantly active, only where his agents attack every soul, is there the slightest hope of moral improvement.

Strange! that a world cursed by God, filled with temptations and thick with fiends, should be the only place where hope exists, the only place where man can repent, the only place where reform is possible! Strange! that heaven, filled with angels and presided over by God, is the only place where reformation is utterly impossible! Yet these are the teachings of all the believers in the eternity of punishment.

Masters frightened slaves with the threat of hell, and slaves got a kind of shadowy revenge by whispering back the threat. The poor have damned the rich and the rich the poor. The imprisoned imagined a hell for their gaolers; the weak built this place for the strong; the arrogant for their rivals; the vanquished for their victors; the priest for the thinker, religion for reason, superstition for science.

All the meanness, all the revenge, all the selfishness, all the cruelty, all the hatred, all the infamy of which the heart of man is capable, grew, blossomed and bore fruit in this one word – hell.

For the nourishment of this dogma cruelty was soil, ignorance was rain, and fear was light.

Christians have placed upon the throne of the universe a God of eternal hate. I cannot worship a being whose vengeance is boundless, whose cruelty is shoreless, and whose malice is increased by the agonies he inflicts.

# The Appeal to the Cemetery

Whoever attacks a custom or a creed, will be confronted with a list of the names of the dead who upheld the custom, or believed the creed. He is asked in a very triumphant and sneering way, if he knows more than all the great and honored of the past Every defender of a creed has graven upon his memory the names of all "great" men whose actions or words can be tortured into evidence for his doctrine. The church is always anxious to have some king or president certify to the moral character of Christ, the authority of the Scriptures, and the justice of the Jewish God. Of late years, confessions of gentlemen about to be hanged have been considered of great value, and the scaffold is regarded as a means of grace.

All the churches of our day seek the rich. They are no longer the friends and defenders of the poor. Poverty no longer feels at home in the house of God. In the Temple of the Most High, garments out of fashion are considered out of place. People now, before confessing to God what worthless souls they have, enrich their bodies. Now words of penitence mingle with the rustle of silk, and light thrown from diamonds adorns the repentant tear. We are told that the rich, the fortunate, the holders of place and office, the fashionable, the respectable, are all within the churches. And yet all these people grow eloquent over the poverty of Christ – boast that he was born in a manger – that the Holy Ghost passed by all the ladies of titled wealth and fashion and selected the wife of a poor and unknown mechanic for the Mother of God.

They admit that all the men of Jerusalem who held high positions – all the people of wealth, influence, and power – were the enemies of the Savior and held his pretensions in contempt. They admit that he had influence only with the poor, and that he was so utterly unknown – so indigent in acquaintance, that it was necessary to bribe one of his disciples to point him out to the police. They assert that he had done a great number of miracles – had cured the sick, and raised the dead – that he had preached to vast multitudes – had made a kind of triumphal entry into Jerusalem – had scourged from the temple the changers of money – had disputed with the doctors – and yet, notwithstanding all these things, he remained in the very depths of obscurity. Surely he and his disciples could have been met with the argument that the "great" dead were opposed to the new religion.

The apostles, it is claimed, preached the doctrines of Christ in Rome and Athens, and the people of those cities could have used the arguments against Christianity that Christians now use in its support. They could have asked the apostles if they were wiser than all the philosophers, poets, orators, and statesmen dead – if they knew more, coming as they did from a weak and barbarous nation, than the greatest men produced by the highest civilization of the known world. With what scorn would the Greeks listen to a barbarian's criticisms upon Socrates[1] and Plato.[2] How a Roman would laugh to hear a vagrant Hebrew attack a mythology that had been believed by Cato[3] and Virgil.[4]

Every new religion has to overcome this argument of the cemetery – this logic of the grave. Old ideas take shelter behind a barricade of corpses and tombstones. They have epitaphs for battlecries, and malign the living in the name of the

---

[1] Socrates (ca. 470-399 B.C.E.), Greek philosopher.

[2] Plato (ca. 428-348 or 347 B.C.E.), Greek philosopher.

[3] Marcus Porcius Cato (234-149 B.C.E.), Roman politician and statesman.

[4] Publius Vergilius Maro (70-19 B.C.E.), known as the greatest of Roman poets.

dead. The moment, however, that a new religion succeeds, it becomes the old religion and uses the same argument against a new idea that it once so gallantly refuted. The arguments used today against what they are pleased to call infidelity would have shut the mouth of every religious reformer, from Christ to the founder of the last sect. The general objection to the new is, that it differs somewhat from the old, and the fact that it does differ is urged as an argument against its truth.

Every man is forced to admit that he does not agree with all the great men, living or dead. The average Catholic, if not a priest, as a rule will admit that Sir Isaac Newton[5] was in some things his superior, that Demosthenes[6] had the advantage of him in expressing his ideas in public, and that as a sculptor he is far below the unknown man of whose hand and brain was born the Venus de Milo, but he will not, on account of these admissions, change his views upon the important question of transubstantiation.

Most Protestants will cheerfully admit that they are inferior in brain and genius to some men who have lived and died in the Catholic Church; that in the matter of preaching funeral sermons they do not pretend to equal Bossuet;[7] that their letters are not so interesting and polished as those of Pascal;[8] that Torquemada[9] excelled them in the genius of organization, and that for planning a massacre they would not for a moment dispute the palm with Catherine de Médici.[10]

---

[5] Sir Isaac Newton (1642-1727), English physicist and mathematician, best known for his conception of the idea of universal gravitation.

[6] Demosthenes (384-322 B.C.E.), Athenian statesman, regarded as the greatest Greek orator.

[7] Jacques-Bénigne Bossuet (1627-1704), French prelate who gained fame as a sermonist.

[8] Blaise Pascal (1623-62), French scientist and philosopher.

[9] Tomás de Torquemada (1420-98), Spanish Dominican monk, served as grand inquisitor and organized the Inquisition in Spain.

[10] Catherine de Médici (1519-89), queen of Henry II of France, was implicated in the St. Bartholomew's Day Massacre (August 23-24, 1572).

And yet, after all these admissions, they would insist that the Pope is an unblushing impostor, and that the Catholic Church is a vampire fattened by the best blood of a thousand years.

The truth is, that in favor of almost every sect, the names of some great men can be pronounced. In almost every church there have been men whose only weakness was their religion, and who in other directions achieved distinction. If you call men great because they were emperors, kings, noblemen, statesmen, millionaires – because they commanded vast armies and wielded great influence in their day, then more names can be found to support and prop the Church of Rome than any other Christian sect.

Is Protestantism willing to rest its claims upon the "great man" argument? Give me the ideas, the religions, not that have been advanced and believed by the so-called great of the past, but that will be defended and believed by the great souls of the future.

It gives me pleasure to say that Lord Bacon[11] was a great man; but I do not for that reason abandon the Copernican system of astronomy, and insist that the earth is stationary. Samuel Johnson[12] was an excellent writer of Latinized English, but I am confident that he never saw a real ghost. Matthew Hale[13] was a reasonably good judge of law, but he was mistaken about witches causing children to vomit crooked pins. John Wesley[14] was quite a man, in a kind of religious way, but in this country few people sympathize with his hatred of republican government, or with his contempt for the Revolutionary Fathers. Sir Isaac Newton, in the domain of science, was the colossus of his time, but his commentary on the Book of Revelation would hardly excite envy, even in the breast of a Spurgeon[15] or a Talmage.[16] Upon many questions,

---

[11] Francis Bacon (1561-1626), English philosopher and author.

[12] Samuel Johnson (1709-84), English writer, lexicographer, and critic.

[13] Sir Matthew Hale (1609-76), English jurist.

[14] John Wesley (1703-91), English religious leader who developed Methodism.

the opinions of Napoleon[17] were of great value, and yet about his bed, when dying, he wanted to see burning the holy candles of Rome. John Calvin[18] has been called a logician, and reasoned well from his premises, but the burning of Servetus[19] did not make murder a virtue. Luther[20] weakened somewhat the power of the Catholic Church, and to that extent was a reformer, and yet Lord Brougham[21] affirmed that his *Table Talk* was so obscene that no respectable English publisher would soil paper with a translation. He was a kind of religious Rabelais;[22] and yet a man can defend Luther in his attack upon the church without justifying his obscenity. If every man in the Catholic Church was a good man, that would not convince me that Ignatius of Loyola[23] ever met and conversed with the Virgin Mary. The fact is, very few men are right in everything.

Great virtues may draw attention from defects, but they cannot sanctify them. A pebble surrounded by diamonds remains a common stone, and a diamond surrounded by pebbles is still a gem. No one should attempt to refute an argument by pronouncing the name of some man, unless he is willing to adopt all the ideas and beliefs of that man. It is better

---

[15] Charles Haddon Spurgeon (1834-92), English Baptist preacher who distrusted modern biblical criticism.

[16] Thomas DeWitt Talmage (1832-1902), American Presbyterian preacher and lecturer.

[17] Napoléon Bonaparte (1769-1821), French emperor.

[18] John Calvin (1509-64), French theologian, established a theocracy in Geneva.

[19] Michael Servetus (1511?-53), Spanish theologian and physician, was burned at the stake by Calvin because he did not accept the Trinity.

[20] Martin Luther (1483-1546), German theologian and founder of Protestantism.

[21] Henry Peter Brougham (1778-1868), British jurist and politician.

[22] François Rabelais (ca. 1483-1553), French writer, known for the racy humor of his novels.

[23] Ignatius of Loyola (1491-1556), Spanish religious, founded the Society of Jesus (Jesuits).

to give reasons and facts than names. An argument should not depend for its force upon the name of its author. Facts need no pedigree; logic has no heraldry, and the living should not be awed by the mistakes of the dead.

The greatest men the world has produced have known but little. They had a few facts, mingled with mistakes without number. In some departments they towered above their fellows, while in others they fell below the common level of mankind.

Daniel Webster[24] had great respect for the Scriptures, but very little for the claims of his creditors. Most men are strangely inconsistent. Two propositions were introduced into the Confederate Congress by the same man. One was to hoist the black flag, and the other was to prevent carrying the mails on Sunday. George Whitefield[25] defended the slave trade, because it brought the negroes within the sound of the gospel, and gave them the advantage of associating with the gentlemen who stole them. And yet this same Whitefield believed and taught the dogma of predestination. Volumes might be written upon the follies and imbecilities of great men. A full rounded man – a man of sterling sense and natural logic – is just as rare as a great painter, poet, or sculptor. If you tell your friend that he is not a painter, that he has no genius for poetry, he will probably admit the truth of what you say, without feeling that he has been insulted in the least. But if you tell him that he is not a logician, that he has but little idea of the value of a fact, that he has no real conception of what evidence is, and that he never had an original thought in his life, he will cut your acquaintance. Thousands of men are most wonderful in mechanics, in trade, in certain professions, keen in business, knowing well the men among whom they live, and yet satisfied with religions infinitely stupid, with politics perfectly senseless, and they will believe that wonderful things were common long ago, such things as no amount of evidence could convince them had happened in their day. A man may be a

---

[24] Daniel Webster (1782-1852), American lawyer and statesman.
[25] George Whitefield (1714-70), English evangelist.

successful merchant, lawyer, doctor, mechanic, statesman, or theologian without one particle of originality, and almost without the ability to think logically upon any subject whatever. Other men display in some directions the most marvelous intellectual power, astonish mankind with their grasp and vigor, and at the same time, upon religious subjects drool and drivel like David at the gates of Gath.[26]

---

[26] 1 Sam. 21:13.

# Sacred Books

We have found, at last, that other nations have sacred books much older than our own, and that these books and records were and are substantiated by traditions and monuments, by miracles and martyrs, christs and apostles, as well as by prophecies fulfilled. In all of these nations differences of opinion as to the authenticity and meaning of these books arose from time to time, precisely as they have done and still do with us, and upon these differences were founded sects that manufactured creeds. These sects denounced each other, and preached with the sword and endeavored to convince with the fagot. Our theologians were greatly astonished to find in other bibles the same stories, precepts, laws, customs, and commands that adorn and stain our own. At first they accounted for this, by saying that these books were in part copies of the Jewish Scriptures, mingled with barbaric myths. To such an extent did they impose upon and insult probability, that they declared that all the morality of the world, all laws commanding right and prohibiting wrong, all ideas respecting the unity of a Supreme Being, were borrowed from the Jews, who obtained them directly from God. The Christian world asserts with warmth, not always born of candor, that the Bible is the source, origin, and fountain of law, liberty, love, charity, and justice; that it is the intellectual and moral sun of the world; that it alone gives happiness here, and alone points out the way to joy hereafter; that it contains the only revelation from the Infinite; that all others are the work of dishonest and mistaken men. They say these things in spite of the fact that the Jewish nation was one of the weakest and most barbaric of the past; in spite of the fact that the civilization of Egypt and India had commenced to wane before that of Palestine existed. To account for all the morality contained in the sacred books of the Hindus by saying that it was borrowed from the wanderers in the Desert of Sinai, from the escaped slaves of the Egyptians, taxes to the utmost the credulity of ignorance, bigotry, and zeal.

The men who make these assertions are not superior to other men. They have only the facts common to all, and they must admit that these facts do not force the same conclusions upon all. They must admit that men equally honest, equally well informed as themselves, deny their premises and conclusions. They must admit that had they been born and educated in some other country, they would have had a different religion, and would have regarded with reverence and awe the books they now hold as false and foolish. Most men are followers, and implicitly rely upon the judgment of others. They mistake solemnity for wisdom, and regard a grave countenance as the title page and preface to a most learned volume. So they are easily imposed upon by forms, strange garments, and solemn ceremonies. And when the teaching of parents, the customs of neighbors, and the general tongue approve and justify a belief or creed, no matter how absurd, it is hard even for the strongest to hold the citadel of his soul. In each country, in defense of each religion, the same arguments would be urged. There is the same evidence in favor of the inspiration of the Koran and Bible. Both are substantiated in exactly the same way. It is just as wicked and unreasonable to be a heretic in Constantinople as in New York. To deny the claims of Christ and Mohammed is alike blasphemous. It all depends upon where you are when you make the denial. No religion has ever fallen that carried with it down to dumb death a solitary fact. Mistakes molder with the temples in which they were taught, and countless superstitions sleep with their dead priests.

Yet Christians insist that the religions of all nations that have fallen from wealth and power were false, with of course the solitary exception of the Jewish, simply because the nations teaching them dropped from their dying hands the

18

swords of power. This argument drawn from the fate of nations proves no more than would one based upon the history of persons. With nations as with individuals, the struggle for life is perpetual, and the law of the survival of the fittest applies equally to both.

It may be that the fabric our civilization will crumbling fall to unmeaning chaos and to formless dust, where oblivion broods and even memory forgets. Perhaps the blind Samson of some imprisoned force, released by thoughtless chance, may so wreck and strand the world that man, in stress and strain of want and fear, will shudderingly crawl back to savage and barbaric night. The time may come in which this thrilled and throbbing earth, shorn of all life, will in its soundless orbit wheel a barren star, on which the light will fall as fruitlessly as falls the gaze of love upon the cold, pathetic face of death.

# Fear

There is a view quite prevalent, that in some way you can prove whether the theories defended or advanced by a man are right or not, by showing what kind of man he was, what kind of life he lived, and what manner of death he died.

A man entertains certain opinions; he is persecuted. He refuses to change his mind, he is burned, and in the midst of flames cries out that he dies without change. Hundreds then say that he has sealed his testimony with his blood, and his doctrines must be true.

All the martyrs in the history of the world are not sufficient to establish the correctness of an opinion. Martyrdom, as a rule, establishes the sincerity of the martyr – never the correctness of his thought. Things are true or false in themselves. Truth cannot be affected by opinions; it cannot be changed, established, or affected by martyrdom. An error cannot be believed sincerely enough to make it a truth.

No Christian will admit that any amount of heroism displayed by a Mormon is sufficient to prove that Joseph Smith was divinely inspired. All the courage and culture, all the poetry and art of ancient Greece, do not even tend to establish the truth of any myth.

The testimony of the dying concerning some other world, or in regard to the supernatural, cannot be any better, to say the least, than that of the living. In the early days of Christianity a serene and intrepid death was regarded as a testimony in favor of the church. At that time Pagans were being converted to Christianity – were throwing Jupiter away and taking the Hebrew God instead. In the moment of death many of these converts, without doubt, retraced their steps and died in the faith of their ancestors. But whenever one died clinging to the cross of the new religion, this was seized upon as an evidence of the truth of the gospel. After a time the Christians taught that an unbeliever, one who spoke or wrote against their doctrines, could not meet death with composure – that the Infidel in his last moments would necessarily be a prey to the serpent of remorse. For more than a thousand years they have made the "facts" to fit this theory. Crimes against men have been considered as nothing when compared with a denial of the truth of the Bible, the divinity of Christ, or the existence of God.

According to the theologians, God has always acted in this way. As long as men did nothing except to render their fellows wretched; as long as they only butchered and burnt the innocent and helpless, God maintained the strictest and most heartless neutrality; but when some honest man, some great and tender soul expressed a doubt as to the truth of the Scriptures, or prayed to the wrong God, or to the right one by the wrong name, then the real God leaped like a wounded tiger upon his victim, and from his quivering flesh tore his wretched soul.

There is no recorded instance where the uplifted hand of murder has been paralyzed – no truthful account in all the literature of the world of the innocent being shielded by God. Thousands of crimes are committed every day – men are this moment lying in wait for their human prey – wives are whipped and crushed, driven to insanity and death – little children begging for mercy, lifting imploring, tear-filled eyes to the brutal faces of fathers and mothers – sweet girls are deceived, lured, and outraged, but God has no time to prevent these things – no time to defend the good and to protect the pure. He is too busy numbering hairs and watching sparrows. He listens for blasphemy; looks for persons who laugh at priests; examines baptismal registers; watches professors in colleges who begin to doubt the geology of Moses and the astronomy of Joshua. He does not particularly object to stealing if you won't swear. A great many persons have fallen dead in the act of taking God's name in vain, but millions of men, women, and children have been stolen from their homes and used as beasts of burden, but no one engaged in this infamy has ever been touched by the wrathful hand of God.

All kinds of criminals, except Infidels, meet death with reasonable serenity. As a rule, there is nothing in the death of a pirate to cast any discredit on his profession. The murderer upon the scaffold, with a priest on either side, smilingly exhorts the multitude to meet him in heaven. The man who has succeeded in making his home a hell, meets death without a quiver, provided he has never expressed any doubt as to the divinity of Christ, or the eternal "procession" of the Holy Ghost. The king who has waged cruel and useless war, who has filled countries with widows and fatherless children, with the maimed and diseased, and who has succeeded in offering to the Moloch of ambition the best and bravest of his subjects, dies like a saint.

The emperor Constantine,[1] who lifted Christianity into power, murdered his wife Fausta,[2] and his eldest son Crispus,[3] the same year that he convened the Council of Nicaea to decide whether Jesus Christ was a man or the Son of God. The council decided that Christ was consubstantial with the Father. This was in the year 325. We are thus indebted to a wife-murderer for settling the vexed question of the divinity of the Savior. Theodosius[4] called a council at Constantinople in 381, and this council decided that the Holy Ghost proceeded from the Father. Theodosius, the younger,[5] assembled another council at Ephesus to ascertain who the Virgin Mary really

---

[1] Constantine I (306-337), Roman emperor.
[2] Flavia Maximiana Fausta (289-326), Roman empress; married Constantine in 307; mother of three emperors.
[3] Flavius Julius Crispus (d. 326), Roman soldier and titular ruler of Gaul.
[4] Theodosius I (347-395), Roman general and emperor (379-395).
[5] Theodosius II (410-450), emperor (408-450).

was, and it was solemnly decided in the year 431 that she was the Mother of God. In 451 it was decided by a council held at Chalcedon, called together by the Emperor Marcian,[6] that Christ had two natures – the human and divine. In 680, in another general council, held at Constantinople, convened by order of Pognatius,[7] it was also decided that Christ had two wills, and in the year 1274 it was decided at the Council of Lyons, that the Holy Ghost proceeded not only from the Father, but from the Son as well. Had it not been for these councils, we might have been without a Trinity even unto this day. When we take into consideration the fact that a belief in the Trinity is absolutely essential to salvation, how unfortunate it was for the world that this doctrine was not established until the year 1274. Think of the millions that dropped into hell while these questions were being discussed.

This, however, is a digression. Let us go back to Constantine. This emperor, stained with every crime, is supposed to have died like a Christian. We hear nothing of fiends leering at him in the shadows of death. He does not see the forms of his murdered wife and son covered with the blood he shed. From his white and shriveled lips issued no shrieks of terror. He does not cover his glazed eyes with thin and trembling hands to shut out the visions of hell. His chamber is filled with the rustle of wings – of wings waiting to bear his soul to the thrilling realms of joy.

Against the emperor Constantine the church has hurled no anathema. She has accepted the story of his vision in the clouds, and his holy memory has been guarded by priest and pope. All the persecutors sleep in peace, and the ashes of those who burned their brothers in the name of Christ rest in consecrated ground. Whole libraries could not contain even the names of the wretches who have filled the world with the violence and death in defense of book and creed, and yet they all died the death of the righteous, and no priest or minister

---

[6] Marcian (ca. 392-457), emperor of the Eastern Roman Empire (450-457).

[7] Constantine IV, called Pogonatius (d. 685), emperor (668-685).

describes the agony and fear, the remorse and horror, with which their guilty souls were filled in the last moments of their lives. These men had never doubted – they accepted the creed – they were not Infidels – they had not denied the divinity of Christ – they had been baptized – they had partaken of the Last Supper – they had respected priests – they admitted that the Holy Ghost had "proceeded," and these things put pillows beneath their dying heads, and covered them with the drapery of peace.

Now and then, in the history of this world, a man of genius, of sense, of intellectual honesty has appeared. These men have denounced the superstitions of their day. They pitied the multitude. To see priests devour the substance of the people filled them with indignation. These men were honest enough to tell their thoughts. Then they were denounced, tried, condemned, executed. Some of them escaped the fury of the people who loved their enemies, and died naturally in their beds.

It would not do for the church to admit that they died peacefully. That would show that religion was not actually necessary in the last moment. Religion got much of its power from the terror of death.

# The Death Test

You had better live well and die wicked. You had better live well and die cursing than live badly and die praying.

It would not do to have the common people understand that a man could deny the Bible, refuse to look at the cross, contend that Christ was only a man, and yet die as calmly as Calvin did after he had murdered Servetus, or as did King David after advising one son to kill another.[1]

The church has taken great pains to show that the last moments of all Infidels (that Christians did not succeed in burning) were infinitely wretched and despairing. It was alleged that words could not paint the horrors that were endured by a dying Infidel. Every good Christian was expected to, and generally did, believe these accounts. They have been told and retold in every pulpit of the world. Protestant ministers have repeated the inventions of Catholic priests, and Catholics, by a kind of theological comity, have sworn to the falsehoods told by Protestants. Upon this point they have always stood together, and will as long as the same calumny can be used by both.

Upon the deathbed subject the clergy grow eloquent. When describing the shudderings and shrieks of the dying unbeliever, their eyes glitter with delight.

It is a festival.

---

[1] In 1 Kings 2:5-6, David instructs his son Solomon to kill Joab, Solomon's cousin.

27

They are no longer men. They become hyenas. They dig open graves. They devour the reputations of the dead.

It is a banquet.

Unsatisfied still, they paint the terrors of hell. They gaze at the souls of the Infidels writhing in the coils of the worm that never dies. They see them in flames – in oceans of fire – in gulfs of pain – in abysses of despair. They shout with joy. They applaud.

It is an *auto da fé,* presided over by God and his angels.

The men they thus describe were not Atheists; they were all believers in God, in special providence, and in the immortality of the soul. They believed in the accountability of man in the practice of virtue, in justice, and liberty, but they did not believe in that collection of follies and fables called the Bible. In order to show that an Infidel must die overwhelmed with remorse and fear, they have generally selected from all the "unbelievers" since the day of Christ five men – the emperor Julian, Spinoza, Voltaire, Diderot, David Hume, and Thomas Paine.

Hardly a minister in the United States has attempted to "answer" me without referring to the death of one or more of these men.

In vain have these calumniators of the dead been called upon to prove their statements. In vain have rewards been offered to any priestly maligner to bring forward the evidence.

Let us once for all dispose of these slanders – of these pious calumnies.

# Julian

They say that the emperor Julian[1] was an "apostate"; that he was once a Christian; that he fell from grace, and that in his last moments, throwing some of his own blood into the air, he cried out to Jesus Christ, "Galilean, thou hast conquered!"

It must be remembered that the Christians had persecuted and imprisoned this very Julian; that they had exiled him; that they had threatened him with death. Many of his relatives were murdered by the Christians. He became emperor, and Christians conspired to take his life. The conspirators were discovered and they were pardoned. He did what he could to prevent the Christians from destroying each other. He held pomp and pride and luxury in contempt, and led his army on foot, sharing the privations of the meanest soldier.

Upon ascending the throne he published an edict proclaiming universal religious toleration. He was then a Pagan. It is claimed by some that he never did entirely forget his Christian education. In this I am inclined to think there is some truth, because he revoked his edict of toleration, and for a time was nearly as unjust as though he had been a saint. He was emperor one year and seven months. In a battle with the Persians he was mortally wounded. "Brought back to his tent, and feeling that he had but a short time to live, he spent his last hours in discoursing with his friends on the immortality of the soul. He reviewed his reign and declared that he was

---

[1] Flavius Claudius Julianus (ca. 331-363), Roman emperor.

satisfied with his conduct, and had neither penitence nor remorse to express for anything that he had done." His last words were: "I submit willingly to the eternal decrees of heaven, convinced that he who is captivated with life, when his last hour has arrived is more weak and pusillanimous than he who would rush to voluntary death when it is his duty still to live."

When we remember that a Christian emperor murdered Julian's father and most of his kindred, and that he narrowly escaped the same fate, we can hardly blame him for having a little prejudice against a church whose members were fierce, ignorant, and bloody – whose priests were hypocrites, and whose bishops were assassins. If Julian had said he was a Christian – no matter what he actually was, he would have satisfied the church.

The story that the dying emperor acknowledged that he was conquered by the Galilean was originated by some of the so-called Fathers of the Church, probably by Gregory[2] or Theodoret.[3] They are the same wretches who said that Julian sacrificed a woman to the moon, tearing out her entrails with his own hands. We are also informed by these hypocrites that he endeavored to rebuild the temple of Jerusalem, and that fire came out of the earth and consumed the laborers employed in the sacrilegious undertaking.

I did not suppose that an intelligent man could be found in the world who believed this childish fable, and yet in the January number for 1880, of the *Princeton Review*, the Rev. Stuart Robinson (whoever he may be) distinctly certifies to the truth of this story. He says: "Throughout the entire era of the planting of the Christian Church, the gospel preached was assailed not only by the malignant fanaticism of the Jew and the violence of Roman statecraft, but also by the intellectual weapons of philosophers, wits, and poets. Now Celsus[4]

---

[2] Gregory I (ca. 540-604), pope (590-604).

[3] Theodoret of Cyrrhus (ca. 393-ca. 458), Greek theologian of the Antioch school.

[4] Celsus (second century C.E.), Roman or Alexandrian philosopher and author of one of the first attacks on Christianity.

denounced the new religion as base imposture. Now Tacitus[5] described it as but another phase of the *odium generis humani*.[6] Now Julian proposed to bring into contempt the prophetic claims of its founder by the practical test of rebuilding the Temple." Here then in the year of grace 1880 is a Presbyterian preacher, who really believes that Julian tried to rebuild the Temple, and that God caused fire to issue from the earth and consume the innocent workmen.

All these stories rest upon the same foundation – the mendacity of priests.

Julian changed the religion of the empire, and diverted the revenues of the church. Whoever steps between a priest and his salary, will find that he has committed every crime. No matter how often the slanders may be refuted, they will be repeated until the last priest has lost his body and found his wings. These falsehoods about Julian were invented some fifteen hundred years ago, and they are repeated today by just as honest and just as respectable people as those who told them at first. Whenever the church cannot answer the arguments of an opponent, she attacks his character. She resorts to falsehood, and in the domain of calumny she has stood for fifteen hundred years without a rival.

The great empire was crumbling to its fall. The literature of the world was being destroyed by priests. The gods and goddesses were driven from the earth and sky. The paintings were torn and defaced. The statues were broken. The walls were left desolate, and the niches empty. Art, like Rachel, wept for her children, and would not be comforted. The streams and forests were deserted by the children of the imagination, and the whole earth was barren, poor and mean.

Christian ignorance, bigotry and hatred, in blind unreasoning zeal, had destroyed the treasures of our race. Art was abhorred, Knowledge was despised, Reason was an outcast. The sun was blotted from the intellectual heaven, every star

---

[5] Cornelius Tacitus (ca. 56-ca. 120), Roman orator, politician, and historian.

[6] *odium generis humani*, hatred of the human race.

extinguished, and there fell upon the world that shadow – that midnight – known as "The Dark Ages."

This night lasted for a thousand years.

The First Great Star – Herald of the Dawn – was Bruno.

# Bruno

The night of the Middle Ages lasted for a thousand years. The first star that enriched the horizon of this universal gloom was Giordano Bruno.[1] He was the herald of the dawn.

He was born in 1550, was educated for a priest, became a Dominican friar. At last his reason revolted against the doctrine of transubstantiation. He could not believe that the entire Trinity was in a wafer, or a swallow of wine. He could not believe that a man could devour the Creator of the universe by eating a piece of bread. This led him to investigate other dogmas of the Catholic Church, and in every direction he found the same contradictions and impossibilities supported, not by reason, but by faith.

Those who loved their enemies threatened his life. He was obliged to flee from his native land, and he became a vagabond in nearly every nation of Europe. He declared that he fought, not what priests believed, but what they pretended to believe. He was driven from his native country because of his astronomical opinions. He had lost confidence in the Bible as a scientific work. He was in danger because he had discovered a truth.

He fled to England. He gave some lectures at Oxford. He found that institution controlled by priests. He found that they were teaching nothing of importance – only the impossible

---

[1] Giordano Bruno (1548-1600), Italian philosopher and mathematician.

33

and the hurtful. He called Oxford "the widow of true learning."
There were in England, at that time, two men who knew more
than the rest of the world. Shakespeare was then alive.

Bruno was driven from England. He was regarded as a
dangerous man – he had opinions, he inquired after reasons,
he expressed confidence in facts. He fled to France. He was not
allowed to remain in that country. He discussed things – that
was enough. The church said, "move on." He went to Germany.
He was not a believer – he was an investigator. The Germans
wanted believers; they regarded the whole Christian system
as settled; they wanted witnesses; they wanted men who
would assert. So he was driven from Germany.

He returned at last to his native land. He found himself
without friends, because he had been true, not only to himself,
but to the human race. But the world was false to him because
he refused to crucify the Christ of his own soul between the
two thieves of hypocrisy and bigotry. He was arrested for
teaching that there are other worlds than this; that many of
the stars are suns, around which other worlds revolve; that
nature did not exhaust all her energies on this grain of sand
called the earth. He believed in a plurality of worlds, in the
rotation of this, in the heliocentric theory. For these crimes,
and for these alone, he was imprisoned for six years. He was
kept in solitary confinement. He was allowed no books, no
friends, no visitors. He was denied pen and paper. In the darkness, in the loneliness, he had time to examine the great questions of origin, of existence, of destiny. He put to the test what
is called the goodness of God. He found that he could neither
depend upon man nor upon any deity. At last, the Inquisition
demanded him. He was tried, condemned, excommunicated
and sentenced to be burned. According to Professor Draper,[2]
he believed that this world is animated by an intelligent soul
– the cause of forms, but not of matter; that it lives in all
things, even in such as seem not to live; that everything is

_____

[2] John William Draper (1811-82), American scientist and author. This
is doubtless a reference to his *History of the Conflict between Religion
and Science* (1874).

ready to become organized; that matter is the mother of forms, and then their grave; that matter and the soul of things, together, constitute God. He was a pantheist – that is to say, an Atheist. He was a lover of nature – a reaction from the asceticism of the church. He was tired of the gloom of the monastery. He loved the fields, the woods, the streams. He said to his brother-priests: Come out of your cells, out of your dungeons: come into the air and light. Throw away your beads and your crosses. Gather flowers; mingle with your fellow men; have wives and children; scatter the seeds of joy; throw away the thorns and nettles of your creeds; enjoy the perpetual miracle of life.

On the sixteenth* day of February, in the year of grace 1600, by "the triumphant beast," the Church of Rome, this philosopher, this great and splendid man, was burned. He was offered his liberty if he would recant. There was no God to be offended by his recantation, and yet, as an apostle of what he believed to be the truth, he refused this offer. To those who passed the sentence upon him he said: "It is with greater fear that ye pass this sentence upon me than I receive it." This man, greater than any naturalist of his day; grander than the martyr of any religion, died willingly in defense of what he believed to be the sacred truth. He was great enough to know that real religion will not destroy the joy of life on earth; great enough to know that investigation is not a crime – that the really useful is not hidden in the mysteries of faith. He knew that the Jewish records were below the level of the Greek and Roman myths; that there is no such thing as special providence; that prayer is useless; that liberty and necessity are the same, and that good and evil are but relative.

He was the first real martyr – neither frightened by perdition, nor bribed by heaven. He was the first of all the world who died for truth without expectation of reward. He did not anticipate a crown of glory. His imagination had not peopled the heavens with angels waiting for his soul. He had not been

---

* It is now generally accepted that Bruno was burned on the seventeenth of February, not the sixteenth.

promised an eternity of joy if he stood firm, nor had he been threatened with the fires of hell if he wavered and recanted. He expected as his reward an eternal nothing! Death was to him an everlasting end – nothing beyond but a sleep without a dream, a night without a star, without a dawn – nothing but extinction, blank, utter, and eternal. No crown, no palm, no "well done, good and faithful servant," no shout of welcome, no song of praise, no smile of God, no kiss of Christ, no mansion in the fair skies – not even a grave within the earth nothing but ashes, wind-blown and priest-scattered, mixed with earth and trampled beneath the feet of men and beasts.

The murder of this man will never be completely and perfectly avenged until from Rome shall be swept every vestige of priest and pope, until over the shapeless ruin of St. Peter's, the crumbled Vatican and the fallen cross, shall rise a monument to Bruno – the thinker, philosopher, philanthropist, Atheist, martyr.

# The Church in the Time of Voltaire

When Voltaire[1] was born, the natural was about the only thing in which the church did not believe. The monks sold little amulets of consecrated paper. They would cure diseases. If laid in a cradle they would prevent a child being bewitched. So, they could be put into houses and barns to keep devils away, or buried in a field to prevent bad weather, to delay frost, and to insure good crops. There was a regular formulary by which they were made, ending with a prayer, after which the amulets were sprinkled with holy water. The church contended that its servants were the only legitimate physicians. The priests cured in the name of the church, and in the name of God, by exorcism, relics, water, salt, and oil. St. Valentine cured epilepsy, St. Gervasius was good for rheumatism, St. Michael de Sanatis for cancer, St. Judas for coughs, St. Ovidius for deafness, St. Sebastian for poisonous bites, St. Apollonia for toothache, St. Clara for rheum in the eye, St. Hubert for hydrophobia. Devils were driven out with wax tapers, with incense, with holy water, by pronouncing prayers. The church, as late as the middle of the twelfth century, prohibited good Catholics from having anything to do with physicians.

It was believed that the devils produced storms of wind, of rain and of fire from heaven; that the atmosphere was a battlefield between angels and devils; that Lucifer had power to destroy fields and vineyards and dwellings, and the principal

---

[1] François-Marie Arouet (1694-1778), pseudonym Voltaire, French satirist, novelist, historian, philosopher.

business of the church was to protect the people from the Devil. This was the origin of church bells. These bells were sprinkled with holy water, and their clangor cleared the air of imps and fiends. The bells also prevented storms and lightning. The church used to anathematize insects. In the sixteenth century, regular suits were commenced against rats, and judgment was rendered. Every monastery had its master magician, who sold magic incense, salt, and tapers, consecrated palms and relics.

Every science was regarded as an outcast, an enemy. Every fact held the creed of the church in scorn. Investigators were enemies in disguise. Thinkers were traitors, and the church exerted its vast power for centuries to prevent the intellectual progress of man. There was no liberty, no education, no philosophy, no science; nothing but credulity, ignorance, and superstition. The world was really under the control of Satan and his agents. The church, for the purpose of increasing her power, exhausted every means to convince the people of the existence of witches, devils, and fiends. In this way the church had every enemy within her power. She simply had to charge him with being a wizard, of holding communication with devils, and the ignorant mob were ready to tear him to pieces.

To such an extent was this frightful course pursued, and such was the prevalence of the belief in the supernatural, that the worship of the devil was absolutely established. The poor people, brutalized by the church, filled with fear of Satanic influence, finding that the church did not protect, as a last resort began to worship the Devil. The power of the Devil was proven by the Bible. The history of Job, the temptation of Christ in the desert, the carrying of Christ to the top of the temple, and hundreds of other instances, were relied upon as establishing his power; and when people laughed about witches riding upon anointed sticks in the air, invisible, they were reminded of a like voyage when the Devil carried Jesus to the pinnacle of the temple.

This frightful doctrine filled every friend with suspicion of his friend. It made the husband denounce the wife, the children the parents, and the parents the children. It destroyed all the sweet relations of humanity. It did away with justice in the courts. It destroyed the charity of religion. It broke the bond of friendship. It filled with poison the golden cup of life. It turned earth into a very hell, peopled with ignorant, tyrannical, and malicious demons.

Such was the result of a few centuries of Christianity. Such was the result of a belief in the supernatural. Such was the result of giving up the evidence of our own senses, and relying upon dreams, visions, and fears. Such was the result of destroying human reason, of depending upon the supernatural, of living here for another world instead of for this, of depending upon priests instead of upon ourselves. The Protestants vied with the Catholics. Luther stood side by side with the priests he had deserted in promoting this belief in devils and fiends. To the Catholic, every Protestant was possessed by a devil. To the Protestant, every Catholic was the homestead of a fiend. All order, all regular succession of causes and effects, were known no more. The natural ceased to exist. The learned and the ignorant were on a level. The priest had been caught in the net spread for the peasant, and Christendom was a vast madhouse, with insane priests for keepers.

When Voltaire was born, the church ruled and owned France. It was a period of almost universal corruption. The priests were mostly libertines. The judges were nearly as cruel as venal. The royal palace was simply a house of assignation. The nobles were heartless, proud, arrogant, and cruel to the last degree. The common people were treated as beasts. It took the church a thousand years to bring about this happy condition of things.

The seeds of the revolution unconsciously were being scattered by every noble and by every priest. They germinated in the hearts of the helpless. They were watered by the tears of agony. Blows began to bear interest. There was a faint longing for blood. Workmen, blackened by the sun, bent by labor, looked at the white throats of scornful ladies and thought about cutting them.

In those days witnesses were cross-examined with instruments of torture. The church was the arsenal of superstition. Miracles, relics, angels, and devils were as common as rags. Voltaire laughed at the evidences, attacked the pretended facts, held the Bible up to ridicule, and filled Europe with indignant protests against the cruelty, bigotry, and injustice of the time.

He was a believer in God, and in some ingenious way excused this God for allowing the Catholic Church to exist. He had an idea that, originally, mankind were believers in one God, and practiced all the virtues. Of course this was a mistake. He imagined that the church had corrupted the human race. In this he was right.

It may be that, at one time, the church relatively stood for progress, but when it gained power, it became an obstruction. The system of Voltaire was contradictory. He described a being of infinite goodness, who not only destroyed his children with pestilence and famine, but allowed them to destroy each other. While rejecting the God of the Bible, he accepted another God, who, to say the least, allowed the innocent to be burned for loving him.

Voltaire hated tyranny and loved liberty. His arguments to prove the existence of a God were just as groundless as those of the reverend fathers of his day to prove the divinity of Christ, or that Mary was the mother of God. The theologians of his time maligned and feared him. He regarded them as a spider does flies. He spread nets for them. They were caught, and he devoured them for the amusement and benefit of the public. He was educated by the Jesuits, and sometimes acted like one.

It is fashionable to say that he was not profound. This is because he was not stupid. In the presence of absurdity he laughed, and was called irreverent. He thought God would not damn even a priest forever: this was regarded as blasphemy. He endeavored to prevent Christians from murdering each other and did what he could to civilize the disciples of Christ. Had he founded a sect, obtained control of some country, and burned a few heretics at slow fires, he would have won the admiration, respect, and love of the Christian world. Had he only pretended to believe all the fables of antiquity, had he mumbled Latin prayers, counted beads, crossed himself, devoured the flesh of God, and carried fagots to the feet of philosophy in the name of Christ, he might have been in heaven this moment, enjoying a sight of the damned.

Instead of doing these things, he willfully closed his eyes to the light of the gospel, examined the Bible for himself, advocated intellectual liberty, struck from the brain the fetters of an arrogant faith, assisted the weak, cried out against the torture of man, appealed to reason, endeavored to establish universal toleration, succored the indigent, and defended the oppressed.

These were his crimes. Such a man God would not suffer to die in peace. If allowed to meet death with a smile, others might follow his example, until none would be left to light the holy fires of the *auto da fé* . It would not do for so great, so successful an enemy of the church, to die without leaving some shriek of fear, some shudder of remorse, some ghastly prayer of chattered horror, uttered by lips covered with blood and foam.

He was an old man of eighty-four. He had been surrounded with the comforts of life; he was a man of wealth, of genius. Among the literary men of the world he stood first. God had allowed him to have the appearance of success. His last years were filled with the intoxication of flattery. He stood at the summit of his age.

The priests became anxious. They began to fear that God would forget, in a multiplicity of business, to make a terrible example of Voltaire.

Toward the last of May, 1778, it was whispered in Paris that Voltaire was dying. Upon the fences of expectation gathered the unclean birds of superstition, impatiently waiting for their prey.

"Two days before his death, his nephew went to seek the curé of Saint Sulpice and the Abbé Gautier and brought them into his uncle's sick chamber, who was informed that they were there. 'Ah, well!' said Voltaire, 'give them my compliments and my

41

thanks.' The Abbé spoke some words to him, exhorting him to patience. The curé of Saint Sulpice then came forward, having announced himself, and asked of Voltaire, elevating his voice, if he acknowledged the divinity of our Lord Jesus Christ. The sick man pushed one of his hands against the curé's coif, shoving him back, and cried, turning abruptly to the other side, 'Let me die in peace.' The curé seemingly considered his person soiled, and his coif dishonored, by the touch of the philosopher. He made the nurse give him a little brushing, and went out with the Abbé Gautier."

He expired, says Wagniere,[2] on the 30th of May, 1778, at about a quarter past eleven at night, with the most perfect tranquility. Ten minutes before his last breath he took the hand of Morand, his *valet de chambre*, who was watching by him, pressed it and said "Adieu, my dear Morand, I am gone." These were his last words.

From the death, so simple and serene, so natural and peaceful; from these words so utterly destitute of cant or dramatic touch, all the frightful pictures, all the despairing utterances, have been drawn and made. From these materials, and from these alone, have been constructed all the shameless lies about the death of this great and wonderful man, compared with whom all of his calumniators, dead and living, were and are but dust and vermin.

Voltaire was the intellectual autocrat of his time. From his throne at the foot of the Alps he pointed the finger of scorn at every hypocrite in Europe. He was the pioneer of his century. He was the assassin of superstition. He left the quiver of ridicule without an arrow. Through the shadows of faith and fable, through the darkness of myth and miracle, through the midnight of Christianity, through the blackness of bigotry, past cathedral and dungeon, past rack and stake, past altar and throne, he carried with chivalric hands, the sacred torch of reason.

---

[2] Wagnière, Voltaire's servant-secretary from 1754-78.

# Diderot

Diderot[1] was born in 1713. His parents were in what may be called the humbler walks of life. Like Voltaire he was educated by the Jesuits. He had in him something of the vagabond, and was for several years almost a beggar in Paris. He was endeavoring to live by his pen. In that day and generation, a man without a patron, endeavoring to live by literature, was necessarily almost a beggar. He nearly starved – frequently going for days without food. Afterward, when he had something himself, he was as generous as the air. No man ever was more willing to give, and no man less willing to receive, than Diderot.

He wrote upon all conceivable subjects, that he might have bread. He even wrote sermons, and regretted it all his life. He and D'Alembert[2] were the life and soul of the *Encyclopaedia*. With infinite enthusiasm he helped to gather the knowledge of the world for the use of each and all. He harvested the fields of thought, separated the grain from the straw and chaff, and endeavored to throw away the seeds and fruit of superstition. His motto was, "Incredulity is the first step toward philosophy."

He had the vices of most Christians – was nearly as immoral as the majority of priests. His vices he shared in common, his virtues were his own. All who knew him united in saying that he had the pity of a woman, the generosity of a

---

[1] Denis Diderot (1713-84), French encyclopedist and philosopher.
[2] Jean Le Rond d'Alembert (1717-83), French mathematician, scientist, and philosopher.

prince, the self-denial of an anchorite, the courage of Caesar, and the enthusiasm of a poet. He attacked with every power of his mind the superstition of his day. He said what he thought. The priests hated him. He was in favor of universal education – the church despised it. He wished to put the knowledge of the whole world within reach of the poorest.

He wished to drive from the gate of the Garden of Eden the cherubim of superstition, so that the child of Adam might return to eat once more the fruit of the tree of knowledge. Every Catholic was his enemy. His poor little desk was ransacked by the police searching for manuscripts in which something might be found that would justify the imprisonment of such a dangerous man. Whoever, in 1750, wished to increase the knowledge of mankind was regarded as the enemy of social order.

The intellectual superstructure of France rests upon the *Encyclopaedia*. The knowledge given to the people was the impulse, the commencement, of the revolution that left the church without an altar and the king without a throne. Diderot thought for himself, and bravely gave his thoughts to others. For this reason he was regarded as a criminal. He did not expect his reward in another world. He did not do what he did to please some imaginary God. He labored for mankind. He wished to lighten the burdens of those who should live after him. Hear these noble words:

> "The more man ascends through the past, and the more he launches into the future, the greater he will be, and all these philosophers and ministers and truth-telling men who have fallen victims to the stupidity of nations, the atrocities of priests, the fury of tyrants, what consolation was left for them in death? This: That prejudice would pass, and that posterity would pour out the vial of ignominy upon their enemies. O Posterity! Holy and sacred stay of the unhappy and the oppressed; thou who art just, thou who art incorruptible, thou who findest the good man, who unmaskest the hypocrite, who breakest down the tyrant, may thy sure faith, thy consoling faith never, never abandon me!"

Posterity is for the philosopher what the other world is for the devotee.

Diderot took the ground that, if orthodox religion be true Christ was guilty of suicide. Having the power to defend himself he should have used it.

Of course it would not do for the church to allow a man to die in peace who had added to the intellectual wealth of the world. The moment Diderot was dead, Catholic priests began painting and recounting the horrors of his expiring moments. They described him as overcome with remorse, as insane with fear; and these falsehoods have been repeated by the Protestant world, and will probably be repeated by thousands of ministers after we are dead. The truth is, he had passed his three-score years and ten. He had lived for seventy-one years. He had eaten his supper. He had been conversing with his wife. He was reclining in his easy chair. His mind was at perfect rest. He had entered, without knowing it, the twilight of his last day. Above the horizon was the evening star, telling of sleep. The room grew still and the stillness was lulled by the murmur of the street. There were a few moments of perfect peace. The wife said, "He is asleep." She enjoyed his repose, and breathed softly that he might not be disturbed. The moments wore on, and still he slept. Lovingly, softly, at last she touched him. Yes, he was asleep. He had become a part of the eternal silence.

# David Hume

The worst religion of the world was the Presbyterianism of Scotland as it existed in the beginning of the eighteenth century The kirk had all the faults of the Church of Rome without a redeeming feature. The kirk hated music, painting, statuary, and architecture. Anything touched with humanity – with the dimples of joy – was detested and accursed. God was to be feared – not loved.

Life was a long battle with the Devil. Every desire was of Satan. Happiness was a snare, and human love was wicked, weak and vain. The Presbyterian priest of Scotland was as cruel, bigoted, and heartless as the familiar of the Inquisition.

Once case will tell it all:

In the beginning of this, the nineteenth century, a boy seventeen years of age, Thomas Aikenhead, was indicted and tried at Edinburgh for blasphemy. He had denied the inspiration of the Bible. He had on several occasions, when cold, jocularly wished himself in hell that he might get warm. The poor, frightened boy recanted – begged for mercy; but he was found guilty, hanged, thrown in a hole at the foot of the scaffold, and his weeping mother vainly begged that his bruised and bleeding body might be given to her.

This one case, multiplied again and again, gives you the condition of Scotland when, on the 26th of April, 1711, David Hume[1] was born.

David Hume was one of the few Scotchmen of his day who were not owned by the church. He had the manliness to examine historical and religious questions for himself, and the

---

[1] David Hume (1711-76), Scottish philosopher and historian.

47

courage to give his conclusions to the world. He was singularly capable of governing himself. He was a philosopher, and lived a calm and cheerful life, unstained by an unjust act, free from all excess, and devoted in a reasonable degree to benefiting his fellow men. After examining the Bible he became convinced that it was not true. For failing to suppress his real opinion, for failing to tell a deliberate falsehood, he brought upon himself the hatred of the church.

Intellectual honesty is the sin against the Holy Ghost, and whether God will forgive this sin or not his church has not, and never will.

Hume took the ground that a miracle could not be used as evidence until the fact that it had happened was established. But *how* can a miracle be established? Take any miracle recorded in the Bible, and *how* could it be established now? You may say: Upon the testimony of those who wrote the account. Who were they? No one knows. How could you prove the resurrection of Lazarus? Or of the widow's son? How could you substantiate, today, the ascension of Jesus Christ? In what way could you prove that the river Jordan was divided upon being struck by the coat of a prophet? How is it possible now to establish the fact that the fires of a furnace refused to burn three men? Where are the witnesses? Who, upon the whole earth, has the slightest knowledge upon this subject?

He insisted that at the bottom of all good was the useful; that human happiness was an end worth working and living for; that origin and destiny were alike unknown; that the best religion was to live temperately and to deal justly with our fellow men; that the dogma of inspiration was absurd, and that an honest man had nothing to fear. Of course the kirk hated him. He laughed at the creed.

To the lot of Hume fell ease, respect, success, and honor. While many disciples of God were the sport and prey of misfortune, he kept steadily advancing. Envious Christians bided their time. They waited as patiently as possible for the horrors of death to fall upon the heart and brain of David Hume. They knew that all the furies would be there, and that God would get his revenge.

48

Adam Smith,[2] author of the *Wealth of Nations*, speaking of Hume in his last sickness, says that in the presence of death "his cheerfulness was so great, and his conversation and amusements ran so much in the usual strain, that, notwithstanding all his bad symptoms, many people could not believe he was dying. A few days before his death Hume said 'I am dying as fast as my enemies – if I have any – could wish, and as easily and tranquilly as my best friends could desire'."

Colonel Edmondstoune shortly afterward wrote Hume a letter, of which the following is an extract:

"My heart is full. I could not see you this morning. I thought it was better for us both. You cannot die – you must live in the memory of your friends and acquaintances; and your works will render you immortal. I cannot conceive that it was possible for any one to dislike you, or hate you. He must be more than savage who could be an enemy to a man with the best head and heart and the most amiable manners."

Adam Smith happened to go into his room while he was reading the above letter, which he immediately showed him. Smith said to Hume that he was sensible of how much he was weakening, and that appearances were in many respects bad; yet, that his cheerfulness was so great and the spirit of life still seemed to be so strong in him, that he could not keep from entertaining some hopes.

Hume answered, "When I lie down in the evening I feel myself weaker than when I arose in the morning; and when I rise in the morning, weaker than when I lay down in the evening. I am sensible, besides, that some of my vital parts are affected so that I must soon die."

"Well," said Mr. Smith, "if it must be so, you have at least the satisfaction of leaving all your friends, and the members of your brother's family in particular, in great prosperity."

He replied that he was so sensible of his situation that when he was reading Lucian's *Dialogues of the Dead,* among all the excuses which are alleged to Charon for not entering

---

[2] Adam Smith (1723-90), Scottish economist.

readily into his boat, he could not find one that fitted him. He had no house to finish; he had no daughter to provide for; he had no enemies upon whom he wished to revenge himself; "and I could not well," said he, "imagine what excuse I could make to Charon in order to obtain a little delay. I have done everything of consequence which I ever meant to do, and I could, at no time expect to leave my relations and friends in a better situation than that in which I am now likely to leave them; and I have, therefore, every reason to die contented."

"Upon further consideration," said he, "I thought I might say to him, 'Good Charon, I have been correcting my works for a new edition. Allow me a little time that I may see how the public receives the alterations.' 'But,' Charon would answer, 'when you have seen the effect of this, you will be for making other alterations. There will be no end to such excuses; so, my honest friend, please step into the boat.' 'But,' I might still urge, 'have a little patience, good Charon; I have been endeavoring to open the eyes of the public; if I live a few years longer, I may have the satisfaction of seeing the downfall of some of the prevailing systems of superstition.' And Charon would then lose all temper and decency, and would cry out. 'You loitering rogue, that will not happen these many hundred years. Do you fancy I will grant you a lease for so long a time? Get into the boat this instant'."

To the Comtesse de Boufflers, the dying man, with the perfect serenity that springs from an honest and loving life writes:

I see death approach gradually without any anxiety or regret. I salute you with great affection and regard, for the last time.

On the 25th of August, 1776, the philosopher, the historian, the Infidel, the honest man, and a benefactor of his race, in the composure born of a noble life, passed quietly and panglessly away.

Dr. Black wrote the following account of his death:

50

Dear Sir:

Yesterday, about four o'clock in the afternoon, Mr. Hume expired. The near approach of his death became evident on the evening between Thursday and Friday, when his disease became exhaustive, and soon weakened him so much that he could no longer rise from his bed. He continued to the last perfectly sensible, and free from much pain or feeling of distress. He never dropped the smallest expression of impatience; but when he had occasion to speak to the people about him, always did it with affection and tenderness.... When he became very weak, it cost him an effort to speak, and he died in such happy composure of mind that nothing could exceed it.

Dr. Cullen writes Dr. Hunter on the 17th of September, 1776, from which the following extracts are made:

You desire an account of Mr. Hume's last days, and I give it to you with great pleasure.... It was truly an example *des grands hommes qui sont morts en plaisantant;* and to me, who have been so often shocked with the horrors of superstition, the reflection on such a death is truly agreeable. For many weeks before his death he was very sensible of his gradual decay; and his answer to inquiries after his health was, several times, that he was going as fast as his enemies could wish, and as easily as his friends could desire. He passed most of the time in his drawing-room, admitting the visits of his friends, and with his usual spirit conversed with them upon literature and politics and whatever else was started. In conversation he seemed to be perfectly at ease; and to the last abounded with that pleasantry and those curious and entertaining anecdotes which ever distinguished him.... His senses and judgment did not fail him to the last hour of his life. He constantly discovered a strong sensibility of the attention and care of his friends; and midst great uneasiness and languor never betrayed any peevishness or impatience." (Here follows the conversation with Charon.) "These are a few particulars which may, perhaps, appear trivial; but to me, no particulars seem trivial which relate to so great a man. It is perhaps from trifles that we can best distinguish the tranquilness and cheerfulness of the philosopher at a time when the most part of mankind are under disquiet, and sometimes even horror. I consider the sacrifice of the cock as a more certain evidence of the tranquillity of Socrates than his discourse on immortality.

The Christians took it for granted that this serene and placid man died filled with remorse for having given his real opinions, and proceeded to describe, with every incident and detail of horror, the terrors of his last moments. Brainless clergymen, incapable of understanding what Hume had written, knowing only in a general way that he had held their creeds in contempt, answered his arguments by maligning his character.

Christians took it for granted that he died in horror and recounted the terrible scenes.

When the facts of his death became generally known to intelligent men, the ministers redoubled their efforts to maintain the old calumnies, and most of them are in this employment even unto this day. Finding it impossible to tell enough falsehoods to hide the truth, a few of the more intelligent among the priests admitted that Hume not only died without showing any particular fear, but was guilty of unbecoming levity. The first charge was that he died like a coward; the next that he did not care enough, and went through the shadowy doors of the dread unknown with a smile upon his lips. The dying smile of David Hume scandalized the believers in a God of love. They felt shocked to see a man dying without fear who denied the miracles of the Bible; who had spent a life investigating the opinions of men; in endeavoring to prove to the world that the right way is the best way; that happiness is a real and substantial good, and that virtue is not a termagant with sunken cheeks and hollow eyes.

Christians hated to admit that a philosopher had died serenely without the aid of superstition one who had taught that man could not make God happy by making himself miserable, and that a useful life, after all, was the best possible religion. They imagined that death would fill such a man with remorse and terror. He had never persecuted his fellow men for the honor of God, and must needs die in despair. They were mistaken.

He died as he had lived. Like a peaceful river with green and shaded banks he passed, without a murmur, into that waveless sea where life at last is rest.

# Benedict Spinoza

One of the greatest thinkers was Benedict Spinoza,[1] a Jew, born at Amsterdam, in 1632. He studied medicine and afterward theology. He endeavored to understand what he studied. In theology he necessarily failed. Theology is not intended to be understood – it is only to be believed. It is an act, not of reason, but of faith. Spinoza put to the rabbis so many questions, and so persistently asked for reasons, that he became the most troublesome of students. When the rabbis found it impossible to answer the questions, they concluded to silence the questioner. He was tried, found guilty, and excommunicated from the synagogue.

By the terrible curse of the Jewish religion, he was made an outcast from every Jewish home. His father could not give him shelter. His mother could not give him bread – could not speak to him, without becoming an outcast herself. All the cruelty of Jehovah, all the infamy of the Old Testament, was in this curse. In the darkness of the synagogue the rabbis lighted their torches, and while pronouncing the curse, extinguished them in blood, imploring God that in like manner the soul of Benedict Spinoza might be extinguished.

Spinoza was but twenty-four years old when he found himself without kindred, without friends, surrounded only by enemies. He uttered no complaint. He earned his bread with willing hands, and cheerfully divided his crust with those still poorer than himself.

---

[1] Baruch Spinoza (1632-77), Dutch philosopher.

He tried to solve the problem of existence. To him, the universe was One. The Infinite embraced the All. The All was God. According to his belief, the universe did not commence to be. It is; from eternity it was; to eternity it will be.

He was right. The universe is all there is, or was, or will be. It is both subject and object, contemplator and contemplated, creator and created, destroyer and destroyed, preserver and preserved, and hath within itself all causes, modes, motions and effects.

In this there is hope. This is a foundation and a star. The Infinite is the All. Without the All, the Infinite cannot be. I am something. Without me, the Infinite cannot exist.

Spinoza was a naturalist – that is to say, a pantheist. He took the ground that the supernatural is, and forever will be, an infinite possibility. His propositions are luminous as stars, and each of his demonstrations is a Gibraltar, behind which logic sits and smiles at all the sophistries of superstition.

Spinoza has been hated because he has not been answered. He was a real republican. He regarded the people as the true and only source of political power. He put the state above the church, the people above the priest. He believed in the absolute liberty of worship, thought, and speech. In every relation of life he was just, true, gentle, patient, modest, and loving. He respected the rights of others, and endeavored to enjoy his own, and yet he brought upon himself the hatred of the Jewish and the Christian world. In his day, logic was blasphemy, and to think was the unpardonable sin. The priest hated the philosopher, revelation reviled reason, and faith was the sworn foe of every fact.

Spinoza was a philosopher, a philanthropist. He lived in a world of his own. He avoided men. His life was an intellectual solitude. He was a mental hermit. Only in his own brain he found the liberty he loved. And yet the rabbis and the priests, the ignorant zealot and the cruel bigot, feeling that this quiet, thoughtful, modest man was in some way forging weapons to be used against the church, hated him with all their hearts.

He did not retaliate. He found excuses for their acts. Their ignorance, their malice, their misguided and revengeful zeal excited only pity in his breast. He injured no man. He did not live on alms. He was poor and yet, with the wealth of his brain, he enriched the world. On Sunday, February 21, 1677, Spinoza, one of the greatest and subtlest of metaphysicians one of the noblest and purest of human beings – at the age of forty-four, passed tranquilly away; and notwithstanding the curse of the synagogue under which he had lived and most lovingly labored, death left upon his lips the smile of perfect peace.

# Our Infidels

In our country there were three Infidels – Paine, Franklin, and Jefferson. The colonies were filled with superstition, the Puritans with the spirit of persecution. Laws savage, ignorant, and malignant had been passed in every colony, for the purpose of destroying intellectual liberty. Mental freedom was absolutely unknown. The Toleration Acts of Maryland tolerated only Christians[1] – not Infidels, not thinkers, not investigators. The charity of Roger Williams[2] was not extended to those who denied the Bible, or suspected the divinity of Christ. It was not based upon the rights of man, but upon the rights of believers, who differed in nonessential points.

The moment the colonies began to deny the rights of the king they suspected the power of the priest. In digging down to find an excuse for fighting George the Third, they unwittingly undermined the church. They went through the Revolution together. They found that all denominations fought equally well. They also found that persons without religion had patriotism and courage, and were willing to die that a new nation might be born. As a matter of fact the pulpit was not in hearty sympathy with our fathers. Many priests were imprisoned because they would not pray for the Continental Congress. After victory had enriched our standard, and it became necessary to make a constitution – to establish a government – the Infidels – the men like Paine, like Jefferson, and like Franklin, saw that the church must be left out; that

---

[1] And only certain Christians. The Toleration Act of 1649 prescribed death and confiscation of property for those who denied the Trinity.
[2] Roger Williams (1603?-83), American clergyman and founder of Rhode Island.

a government deriving its just powers from the consent of the governed could make no contract with a church pretending to derive its powers from an infinite God.

By the efforts of these Infidels, the name of God was left out of the Constitution of the United States. They knew that if an infinite being was put in, no room would be left for the people. They knew that if any church was made the mistress of the state, that mistress, like all others, would corrupt, weaken, and destroy. Washington wished a church established by law in Virginia. He was prevented by Thomas Jefferson. It was only a little while ago that people were compelled to attend church by law in the eastern states, and taxes were raised for the support of churches the same as for the construction of highways and bridges. The great principle enunciated in the Constitution has silently repealed most of these laws. In the presence of this great instrument, the constitutions of the States grew small and mean, and in a few years every law that puts a chain upon the mind, except in Delaware, will be repealed, and for these our children may thank the Infidels of 1776.

The church never has pretended that Jefferson or Franklin died in fear. Franklin wrote no books against the fables of the ancient Jews. He thought it useless to cast the pearls of thought before the swine of ignorance and fear. Jefferson was a statesman. He was the father of a great party. He gave his views in letters and to trusted friends. He was a Virginian, author of the Declaration of Independence, founder of a university, father of a political party, president of the United States, a statesman and philosopher. He was too powerful for the divided churches of his day. Paine was a foreigner, a citizen of the world. He had attacked Washington and the Bible. He had done these things openly, and what he had said could not be answered. His arguments were so good that his character was bad.

# Thomas Paine

Thomas Paine[1] was born in Thetford, England. He came from the common people. At the age of thirty-seven he left England for America. He was the first to perceive the destiny of the New World. He wrote the pamphlet *Common Sense*, and in a few months the Continental Congress declared the colonies free and independent states – a new nation was born. Paine having aroused the spirit of independence, gave every energy of his soul to keep the spirit alive. He was with the army. He shared its defeats and its glory. When the situation became desperate, he gave them *The Crisis*. It was a pillar of cloud by day and of fire by night, leading the way to freedom, honor, and to victory.

The writings of Paine are gemmed with compact statements that carry conviction to the dullest. Day and night he labored for America, until there was a government of the people and for the people. At the close of the Revolution, no one stood higher than Thomas Paine. Had he been willing to live a hypocrite, he would have been respectable, he at least could have died surrounded by other hypocrites, and at his death there would have been an imposing funeral, with miles of carriages, filled with hypocrites, and above his hypocritical dust there would have been a hypocritical monument covered with lies.

Having done so much for man in America, he went to France. The seeds sown by the great Infidels were bearing fruit in Europe. The eighteenth century was crowning its gray

---

[1] Thomas Paine (1737-1809), political philosopher and revolutionary.

hairs with the wreath of progress. Upon his arrival in France he was elected a member of the French Convention – in fact, he was selected about the same time by the people of no less than four departments. He was one of the committee to draft a constitution for France. In the Assembly, where nearly all were demanding the execution of the king, he had the courage to vote against death. To vote against the death of the king was to vote against his own life. This was the sublimity of devotion to principle. For this he was arrested, imprisoned, and doomed to death. While under sentence of death, while in the gloomy cell of his prison, Thomas Paine wrote to Washington, asking him to say one word to Robespierre[2] in favor of the author of *Common Sense*. Washington did not reply. He wrote again. Washington, the president, paid no attention to Thomas Paine, the prisoner. The letter was thrown into the wastebasket of forgetfulness, and Thomas Paine remained condemned to death. Afterward he gave his opinion of Washington at length, and I must say, that I have never found it in my heart to greatly blame him.

Thomas Paine, having done so much for political liberty, turned his attention to the superstitions of his age. He published *The Age of Reason*; and from that day to this, his character has been maligned by almost every priest in Christendom. He has been held up as the terrible example. Every man who has expressed an honest thought, has been warningly referred to Thomas Paine. All his services were forgotten. No kind word fell from any pulpit. His devotion to principle, his zeal for human rights, were no longer remembered. Paine simply took the ground that it is a contradiction to call a thing a revelation that comes to us secondhand. There can be no revelation beyond the first communication. All after that is hearsay. He also showed that the prophecies of the Old Testament had no relation whatever to Jesus Christ, and contended that Jesus Christ was simply a man. In other words, Paine was an enlightened Unitarian. Paine thought the Old

---

[2] Maximilien-François-Marie-Isidore de Robespierre (1758-94), French revolutionist, responsible for much of the "Reign of Terror."

Testament too barbarous to have been the word of an infinitely benevolent God. He attacked the doctrine that salvation depends upon belief. He insisted that every man has the right to think.

After the publication of these views every falsehood that malignity could coin and malice pass was given to the world. On his return to America, after the election to the presidency of another Infidel, Thomas Jefferson, it was not safe for him to appear in the public streets. He was in danger of being mobbed. Under the very flag he had helped to put in heaven his rights were not respected. Under the Constitution that he had suggested, his life was insecure. He had helped to give liberty to more than three millions of his fellow citizens, and they were willing to deny it unto him. He was deserted, ostracized, shunned, maligned, and cursed. He enjoyed the seclusion of a leper; but he maintained through it all integrity. He stood by the convictions of his mind. Never for one moment did he hesitate or waver.

He died almost alone. The moment he died Christians commenced manufacturing horrors for his deathbed. They had his chamber filled with devils rattling chains, and these ancient lies are annually certified to by the respectable Christians of the present day. The truth is, he died as he had lived. Some ministers were impolite enough to visit him against his will. Several of them he ordered from his room. A couple of Catholic priests, in all the meekness of hypocrisy, called that they might enjoy the agonies of a dying friend of man. Thomas Paine, rising in his bed, the few embers of expiring life blown into flame by the breath of indignation, had the goodness to curse them both. His physician, who seems to have been a meddling fool, just as the cold hand of death was touching the patriot's heart, whispered in the dull ear of the dying man: "Do you believe, or do you wish to believe, that Jesus Christ is the son of God?" And the reply was: "I have no wish to believe on that subject."

These were the last remembered words of Thomas Paine. He died as serenely as ever Christian passed away. He died in the full possession of his mind, and on the very brink and edge of death proclaimed the doctrines of his life.

Every Christian, every philanthropist, every believer in human liberty, should feel under obligation to Thomas Paine for the splendid service rendered by him in the darkest days of the American Revolution. In the midnight of Valley Forge, *The Crisis* was the first star that glittered in the wide horizon of despair. Every good man should remember with gratitude the brave words spoken by Thomas Paine in the French Convention against the death of Louis. He said: "We will kill the king, but not the man. We will destroy monarchy, not the monarch."

Thomas Paine was a champion, in both hemispheres, of human liberty; one of the founders and fathers of this Republic; one of the foremost men of his age. He never wrote a word in favor of injustice. He was a despiser of slavery. He abhorred tyranny in every form. He was, in the widest and best sense, a friend of all his race. His head was as clear as his heart was good, and he had the courage to speak his honest thought.

He was the first man to write these words: "The United States of America." He proposed the present federal Constitution. He furnished every thought that now glitters in the Declaration of Independence.

He believed in one God and no more. He was a believer even in special providence, and he hoped for immortality.

How can the world abhor the man who said:

"I believe in the equality of man, and that religious duties consist in doing justice, in loving mercy, and endeavoring to make our fellow creatures happy."

"It is necessary to the happiness of man that he be mentally faithful to himself."

"The word of God is the creation which we behold."

"Belief in a cruel God makes a cruel man."

"My opinion is, that those whose lives have been spent in doing good and endeavoring to make their fellow mortals happy, will be happy hereafter."

62

"One good schoolmaster is of more use than a hundred priests."

"I believe in one God, and no more, and I hope for happiness beyond this life."

"Man has no property in man."

"The key of heaven is not in the keeping of any sect!"

Had it not been for Thomas Paine I could not deliver this lecture here to-night.

It is still fashionable to calumniate this man – and yet Channing,[3] Theodore Parker,[4] Longfellow,[5] Emerson,[6] and in fact all the liberal Unitarians and Universalists of the world have adopted the opinions of Thomas Paine.

Let us compare these Infidels with the Christians of their time:

Compare Julian with Constantine – the murderer of his wife – the murderer of his son – and who established Christianity with the same sword he had wet with their blood. Compare him with all the Christian emperors – with all the robbers and murderers and thieves – the parricides and fratricides and matricides that ever wore the imperial purple on the banks of the Tiber or the shores of the Bosphorus.

Let us compare Bruno with the Christians who burned him; and we will compare Spinoza, Voltaire, Diderot, Hume, Jefferson, Paine – with the men who it is claimed have been the visible representatives of God.

Let it be remembered that the popes have committed every crime of which human nature is capable, and that not one of them was the friend of intellectual liberty – that not one of them ever shed one ray of light.

Let us compare these Infidels with the founders of sectarian churches; you will see how narrow, how bigoted, how cruel

---

3 William Ellery Channing (1780-1842), American clergyman who became known as the "apostle of Unitarianism."

4 Theodore Parker (1810-60), American clergyman known for his liberal stance.

5 Henry Wadsworth Longfellow (1807-82), American poet.

6 Ralph Waldo Emerson (1803-82), American essayist and poet.

were their founders, and how broad, how generous, how noble, were these Infidels.

Let us be honest. The great effort of the human mind is to ascertain the order of facts by which we are surrounded – the history of things.

Who has accomplished the most in this direction – the church, or the unbelievers? Upon one side write all that the church has discovered – every phenomenon that has been explained by a creed, every new fact in nature that has been discovered by a church, and on the other side write the discoveries of Humboldt,[7] and the observations and demonstrations of Darwin![8]

Who has made Germany famous – her priests, or her scientists?

Goethe.[9]

Kant:[10] That immortal man who said: "Whoever thinks that he can please God in every way except by discharging his obligations to his fellows, is superstitious."

And that greatest and bravest of thinkers, Ernst Haeckel.[11]

Humboldt.

Italy: Mazzini.[12] Garibaldi.[13]

In France who are and were the friends of freedom – the Catholic priests, or Renan?[14] The bishops, or Gambetta?[15] Dupanloup,[16] Or Victor Hugo?[17]

---

[7] Alexander von Humboldt (1769-1859), German naturalist, traveler, and statesman.

[8] Charles Robert Darwin (1809-82), English naturalist and originator of the natural selection theory of evolution.

[9] Johann Wolfgang von Goethe (1749-1832), German poet, scientist, and dramatist.

[10] Immanuel Kant (1724-1804), German philosopher.

[11] Ernst Haeckel (1834-1919), German biologist and philosopher.

[12] Giuseppe Mazzini (1805-72), Italian patriot and revolutionary.

[13] Giuseppe Garibaldi (1807-82), Italian patriot.

[14] Joseph-Ernest Renan (1823-92), French philosopher, philologist, and historian.

[15] Léon-Michel Gambetta (1838-82), French politician.

Michelet[18] – Taine[19] – Auguste Comte.[20]

England: Let us compare her priests with John Stuart Mill[21] – Harriet Martineau,[22] that "free rover on the breezy common of the universe" – George Eliot[23] – with Huxley[24] and Tyndall,[25] with Holyoake[26] and Harrison[27] – and above and overall – with Charles Darwin.

---

[16] Felix-Antoine-Philibert Dupanloup (1802-78), French prelate and politician.

[17] Victor-Marie Hugo (1802-85), French novelist, dramatist, and poet.

[18] Jules Michelet (1798-1874), French historian.

[19] Hippolyte-Adolphe Taine (1828-93), French philosopher, historian, and critic.

[20] Auguste Comte (1798-1857), French philosopher, founder of positivism and of sociology.

[21] John Stuart Mill (1806-73), English philosopher, economist, and women's suffragist.

[22] Harriet Martineau (1802-76), English Atheist, economist, abolitionist, and novelist.

[23] Mary Ann Evans (1819-80), pseudonym George Eliot, English novelist.

[24] Thomas Henry Huxley (1825-95), English biologist, evolutionist, philosopher.

[25] John Tyndall (1820-93), Irish physicist.

[26] George Jacob Holyoake (1817-1906), English reformer and Atheist leader.

[27] Frederic Harrison (1831-1923), English positivist philosopher.

# Conclusion

Let us be honest. Did all the priests of Rome increase the mental wealth of man as much as Bruno? Did all the priests of France do as great a work for the civilization of the world as Diderot and Voltaire? Did all the ministers of Scotland add as much to the sum of human knowledge as David Hume? Have all the clergymen, monks, friars, ministers, priests, bishops, cardinals, and popes, from the day of Pentecost to the last election, done as much for human liberty as Thomas Paine? As much for science as Charles Darwin?

What would the world be if Infidels had never been?

The Infidels have been the brave and thoughtful men; the flower of all the world; the pioneers and heralds of the blessed day of liberty and love; the generous spirits of the unworthy past; the seers and prophets of our race; the great chivalric souls, proud victors on the battlefields of thought, the creditors of all the years to be.

Why should it be taken for granted that the men who devoted their lives to the liberation of their fellow men should have been hissed at in the hour of death by the snakes of conscience, while men who defended slavery, practiced polygamy, justified the stealing of babes from the breasts of mothers, and lashed the naked back of unpaid labor are supposed to have passed smilingly from earth to the embraces of the angels? Why should we think that the brave thinkers, the investigators, the honest men, must have left the crumbling shore of time in dread and fear, while the instigators of the massacre of St. Bartholomew; the inventors and users of thumbscrews, of iron boots and racks; the burners and tearers of human flesh; the stealers, the whippers and the enslavers of men; the buyers and beaters of maidens, mothers, and babes; the founders of the Inquisition; the makers of chains; the builders of dungeons; the calumniators of the living; the slanderers of the dead, and even the murderers of Jesus Christ, all died in the odor of sanctity, with white, forgiven hands folded upon the breasts of peace, while the destroyers of prejudice, the apostles of humanity, the soldiers of liberty, the breakers of fetters, the creators of light, died surrounded by the fierce fiends of God?